All Awesome Toddler Recipes

An Inspiring Cookbook with Toddler M

and Many Fun Tips

BY - Charlotte Long

License Page

No part of this book and its content should be transmitted in any format for commercial and personal use without asking for permission from the author in writing.

The purpose of the content is to enlighten you and pass cooking knowledge to you in a straightforward way. Hence, the author is not responsible for any implications and assumptions drawn from the book and its content.

Table of Contents

Introduction

Let's first clear up what ages are included in the term toddlers. A toddler is a child between 1 year old and 3 years old. Now that this is established let's talk about their needs daily nutritionally wise.

It seems like toddlers often lack Vitamin D, calcium, fiber, and potassium in their regular diet, so let's emphasize giving them enough of those and more.

We suggest your toddler gets just about 1000 calories a day. You should aim to feed them 3 meals and a few snacks a day. Like you should aim for yourself.

These meals should contain about 1 cup of vegetables and 1 cup of fruits overall. It should contain about 1.2 cups of grains and just about 2 cups of dairy products. Finally, but not lastly, make sure your toddler gets at least 2 ounces of proteins and plenty of healthy fats.

So, here is how you should build a toddler's meal or plate. Just make it easy on yourself and include a little of each food group. Half of the plate will be built with fruits and veggies, and the other half will be split between proteins and grains. Add a serving of dairy on the side (maybe yogurt or a glass of milk) unless you already added some cheese on the plate. Make sure you give your toddler whole milk products until 2 or 3. They need the extra fat and will burn it quickly.

Don't get discouraged! Offer your little one the same food many times, even when their first resists. You can play with the way you serve it, the texture (puree, cooked, raw), and even camouflage it within other foods (cauliflower in mashed potatoes). Exploring textures as much as tastes is important for toddlers. Also, try to sit down with your child each time he eats, so he knows and develops these social eating habits also and manners at the table.

Do not allow screen time while they are eating. No tablet, no TV, no cell phone. Kids should focus on eating and maybe having a "conversation" at the table, but it's not playtime or distracting time. Also, although you may need to customize their plate, you should aim for your toddler to eat the same main foods as the rest of the family. This will make it easier for you. Sure, you may be based on sweet potatoes for everyone else, but just serve your toddler some mashes.

Ensure that the snacks also respect these healthy rules and are not too filling or close to mealtimes, so they don't spoil their lunch or dinner. Also, avoid giving them a lot of juices or milk before meals. Stick to water anyways as much as possible, or at least sugar-free juices.

Do not force your toddler to eat. Don't shuffle food in their mouth. They will associate eating with a stressful and unpleasant experience, and that's the last thing you want them to do. Also, they won't always have to finish their plate. Some days or meals they will, and some they won't.

1. Parmesan Crusted Chicken Bites

It's important to remember that processed food is not as good as homemade. If you are going to serve chicken nuggets or chicken fingers to your toddlers, make sure you make them from scratch. Use some chicken breasts and some homemade breading.

Serving Size: 4-6

Cooking Time: 40 Minutes

Ingredients:

- 3 skinless and boneless chicken breasts
- ½ cup powdered Parmesan cheese
- ½ cup panko breadcrumbs
- 1 large egg
- ¼ cup whole milk
- Salt, black pepper
- ¼ tsp. ground nutmeg
- Frying oil

Instructions:

Clean the chicken breast and cut it into nuggets pieces.

Combine the nutmeg, breadcrumbs, pepper, salt, and Parmesan cheese in a medium bowl.

In a second bowl, combine the milk and egg.

In a large pan, heat the oil at a high temperature.

Take each piece of chicken and dip it on the milk mixture and then in the breadcrumb's mixture.

Cook in the hot oil. Make sure it's completely done before removing it from heat.

Place on paper towels and let the excess oil absorb.

Serve warm with your little one's favorite dip.

2. Mini Chicken Salad Sandwiches

These sandwiches can be made in no time. When you have leftover chicken make sure you look at all the options to use up that chicken. Preparing ahead chicken salad with mayonnaise, the right spices, and perhaps some celery or cucumbers will allow you to use that spread on bread or crackers.

Serving Size: 2-4

Cooking Time: 15 Minutes

Ingredients:

- 1 cup cooked chicken
- 2 tbsp. mayonnaise
- 1 diced celery stalk
- 1 tbsp. diced onions (you can skip if your toddler won't like it)
- Pinch ground cumin
- Salt and black pepper
- 4-6 Sandwich bread slices

Instructions:

Combine the mayonnaise, spices, celery, and onion in a large bowl.

Make sure it's not too spicy after tasting it.

Add the cooked chicken.

Get the sliced bread out. I suggest you pick whole grains, so it's healthier.

Spread the chicken mixture on the bread, cut the sandwich into triangles or squares, and serve with a side of seedless grapes or sliced apples.

Remember how you cut the sandwiches can make a big difference in how much they are interested in eating their food. You can use the cookie cutter to make fun shapes for the little ones.

3. The Cheesiest Grilled Cheese Sandwich

Most kids and most toddlers have in common that they love cheese. Hopefully, yours doesn't have any lactose intolerant and is as happy as mine to see cheese on their plate. If they are, then it's time to make this cheesiest grilled cheese sandwich you have ever tasted!

Serving Size: 2

Cooking Time: 15 Minutes

Ingredients:

- 4 slices American cheese
- 4 slices sourdough or Italian white bread
- Unsalted butter

Instructions:

Butter each slice of bread.

Heat a large pan to medium-high temperature.

Add 2 slices of cheese to each sandwich, and you want it to be cheesy.

Place in the hot pan and cook on one side for 4-5 minutes. Use a spatula to press the sandwich. Flip over and repeat.

Make sure you keep the temperature low enough, so it does not burn.

When done, cut into small bites and serve with fresh-cut broccoli and ranch sauce. You can also choose to serve with a fruit salad on the side.

4. Tater Tots Casserole on Stovetop

When you make a casserole, it does not have to be in the oven. I learned that much. I also understand that it can be delicious and simple at the same time. Simple is good when you serve toddlers because they are usually starving when you're ready to cook!

Serving Size: 4

Cooking Time: 30-35 Minutes

Ingredients:

- 16 ounces frozen taster tots (thawed)
- 1 cup mild salsa
- 2 cups kernel corn
- 2 cups shredded Mozzarella cheese
- Olive oil
- Salt, black pepper

Instructions:

In a large pan, heat some oil and add the tater tots. Sauté.

They need to stay crunchy, so stir often.

In a mixing bowl, combine the salsa, cheese, and corn. Season with salt and a little pepper if you judge it appropriately.

After a good 30-25 minutes, add the mixture to the tots.

Combine well. Reduce the heat and let the cheese melt and ingredients warm up.

Then it's ready to be served! This can be a full meal if you ever want to add cooked chicken or tuna.

5. Honey Warm Baby Carrots

Carrots are rather sweet. Toddlers like sweet and colorful food. So usually, toddlers happily welcome baby carrots. Add some honey to the mix, and you're almost certain that your toddlers will love this dish.

Serving Size: 6-8

Cooking Time: 50-60 Minutes

Ingredients:

- 2 cups fresh baby carrots
- 1.2 cups honey
- ½ cup water
- Pinch of fresh rosemary
- ½ tsp. salt

Instructions:

In a medium pot, pour the honey and water.

Bring to boil.

Add the carrots and cook for about 12-15 minutes.

You want to keep them slightly crunchy.

If you think you next more water, add more.

Once done, drain carefully.

Sprinkle a little rosemary and salt. Again, you know your toddler better. Perhaps the rosemary is too strong a dried Italian seasonings will be more suited.

Serve with their favorite meat of fish.

6. Pancakes, Maple Syrup, and Coconut Oil

Pancakes are often a desirable breakfast item to make for your toddlers. Sure, they are delicious, and they are fluffy, and they are rather easy to make. Also, you can make pancakes what extra nutritious ingredients, such as chia seeds, coconut oil, and more.

Serving Size: 4

Cooking Time: 20-25 Minutes

Ingredients:

- Coconut oil for cooking
- 11/2 cup coconut flour
- 1 medium egg
- 2 tbsp. chia seeds
- ½ cup whole milk
- ¼ tsp. vanilla extract
- ½ tsp. baking soda
- Pinch salt
- Maple syrup, for serving

Instructions:

Combine the flour, chia seeds, baking soda, and salt in a medium bowl.

In a second bowl, combine the egg, milk, and vanilla.

Dump the wet mixture into the dried ones.

Combine well. Heat the coconut oil in a medium pan on medium heat.

Dump a large tablespoon of batter at a time in the hot pan.

Cook as many pancakes as you can.

Make sure you flip them over after about 3-4 minutes. The other side will cook faster.

Serve your toddler as many pancakes as they want.

Don't forget to suggest maple syrup on top! Or, if you are really daring, sprinkle some roasted shaved coconut on top!

7. Blueberries and Yogurt Popsicles

Having popsicles ready to grab for your toddlers on a hot day seems like a good idea. Buying popsicles from the store made with only sugared water is not such a great idea that your toddlers don't need more artificial sugars. That's why I love this recipe. It combines fresh fruits and yogurt.

Serving Size:8-12**Cooking Time:** 20 Minutes

Ingredients:

- 2 cups fresh blueberries
- 3 cups Greek plain yogurt
- 1 tbsp. agave syrup
- 1 cup ice

Instructions:

Get your blender out and your popsicles molds.

Wash and carefully drain the fresh blueberries.

Add half of all ingredients to the blender.

Activate until the mixture is smooth.

Dump the first half of the mixture into the popsicle's molds.

Repeat with the rest of the ingredients and fill up the molds.

Freeze for at least 2 hours before serving.

Although they are healthier, they will still melt! So, make sure you supervise your toddler when eating to avoid messes.

8. Fun Ideas of Peanut Butter on Celery

I remember vividly fighting to eat salary as a kid. I did not like this taste then; I still don't like the taste or texture of the celery. But there was one way my mom could make me tolerate the salary is when she spread some peanut butter on it. Let's see what else we can add!

Serving Size: 6-8

Cooking Time: 50-60 Minutes

Ingredients:

- 2-3 celery stalks
- 2 tbsp. peanut butter
- 4 red apple slices
- 4-6 green and red seedless grapes
- 4 pretzel pieces

Instructions:

Wash the celery carefully and let it dry.

Also, wash the grapes and cut them in halves.

Cut the celery into 3-4 pieces. Spread peanut butter into the middle, generously.

Use the pretzels and grapes to create bug-looking celery.

You may have to break the pretzels and use your imagination.

Do it with your toddler!

I have made this fun celery before by replacing the peanut butter with almond butter. I have also made these with cream cheese instead of peanut butter.

9. Spinach and Feta Fried Balls

Feta and spinach do go well together. You can mix them up in an omelet or a salad, but I guarantee your toddlers will love these fried tasty balls. They will be able to grab them quickly with their little hands and dip them into whatever dipping sauce you choose to serve them with.

Serving Size: 12

Cooking Time: 40-45 Minutes

Ingredients:

- 2 cups panko crumbs
- 1 large egg
- 2 cups crumbled Feta cheese
- 8 ounces pancake plain cream cheese
- 1 (12 ounces) package of chopped spinach (frozen and thawed)
- ½ tsp. smoked paprika
- Frying oil

Instructions:

Make sure the spinach is well-drained before using.

Combine the combine both cheeses (cream cheese and Feta), spinach, and egg in a large mixing bowl. Add also the smoked paprika.

Heat the oil at a high temperature since you are going to fry these balls.

Form small balls with the cheese mixture and dip them in the breadcrumbs mixture to coat completely.

Put in the hot oil and cook for about 6-7 minutes or until nice and golden.

Let them cool down before serving to your toddler.

Grease a 12 holes muffin tin and set it aside.

Dump the final mixture into the muffin holes and bake for 40 minutes or so.

Let the muffins cool down and pack them in your lunches any day!

10. A Spaghetti Is Always a Winner

Remember when I said to keep things simple? Spaghetti is simple enough. But because you decide to serve pasta doesn't mean you'd have to limit yourself to spaghetti noodles! You can change it up and use some shells pasta, rotini, linguine, macaroni, or any other type and shape of paste you think your toddler will enjoy.

Serving Size: 4

Cooking Time: 25-30 Minutes

Ingredients:

- 2 cups cooked spaghetti or pasta noodles of your choice
- ¾ cup of Parmesan cheese or Mozzarella cheese
- ½ cup spaghetti sauce or tomato sauce your toddler likes

Instructions:

Simply portion the noodles and sauce according to your toddler's preference.

I usually cut the spaghetti noodles into 3, 4 so it's easier for the little one to eat.

Add the sauce on top. Some kids like more or less.

Add the cheese they also like and place it in the microwave but ensure it's not too hot when serving.

11. The Meatballs Toddlers Love

Meatballs or rather easy to make. They are, however, time-consuming. So next time you make a batch of meatballs, make extra and freeze them. Then, all you have to do is either reheat them or make a sauce to serve them to your toddler. Serve a side of veggies with it, and you have a complete meal.

Serving Size: 4

Cooking Time: 50-60 Minutes

Ingredients:

- 1 ½ pound of meat or turkey ground meat
- 1 large egg
- 2/3 cup Italian seasoned breadcrumbs
- ½ tsp. garlic, minced
- ½ tsp. onion powder
- 2-3 cups tomato sauce or alfredo sauce, your preference

Instructions:

Preheat the oven to 400°F.

Grease a baking sheet and set it aside.

Combine the onion powder, garlic, meat, breadcrumbs, and egg in a mixing bowl.

Use your hands to mix well.

Form small meatballs and place them on the baking sheet.

Bake in the oven for 40-45 minutes or until done.

You can serve these with or without sauce.

Choose the sauce you know your toddler will prefer.

Also, if you do serve in sauce, you can put them in halves or quarters and let them eat it like a soup with a spoon.

You could also create a gratin dish by placing the meatballs and sauce in a baked dish and adding a layer of Mozzarella cheese to broil for 5 minutes.

12. Simple Black Beans Patties

You have to be able to balance off spices. Black beans go well with cumin but don't use too much because toddlers might not be crazy about the flavor. They will, however, always wake welcome patties that are easy to grab, and they are easy to serve as a sandwich.

Serving Size:4-8

Cooking Time: 30- Minutes

Ingredients:

- 1 large can of black beans (12 ounces)
- 1 large egg
- ½ cup panko breadcrumbs
- ¾ cup shredded cheddar cheese
- ¼ tsp. ground cumin
- ¼ tsp. ground nutmeg
- ¼ tsp. salt
- Olive oil to cook

Instructions:

Drain the black beans well. Place in a large mixing bowl.

Add all the other ingredients.

Use your hands to mix. Make sure all ingredients are well-combined.

Form patties and make them smaller because remember these are for toddlers. If you want to make a few bigger ones for any adults in your household, go for it!

Heat the oil to medium-high.

Cook the patties on each side. It should take you a total of 15 minutes.

Place the cooked patties on paper towels to ensure excess oil gets absorbed.

Cut them in pieces when serving to toddlers. Or you can make sandwiches if you want. Perhaps use these tiny Hawaiian buns to serve them.

13. Delicious Cheese Biscuits

You can serve these yummy cheese biscuits for breakfast or as a side bread with your toddler's pasta lunch. But most importantly, you do make these goodies from scratch and with lots of nutritious cheese and can pack them easily when going to the park.

Serving Size:12-16

Cooking Time: 40- Minutes

Ingredients:

- 2 cups all-purpose flour
- ¾ cup whole milk
- ½ tsp. baking soda
- 1 medium egg
- 1 cup shredded orange American or Cheddar cheese
- ½ tsp. baking powder
- ¼ tsp. salt
- Pinch ground nutmeg
- ¼ melted cup Unsalted butter

Instructions:

Preheat the oven to 350°F.

Grease a baking sheet and set aside. I also like to use parchment paper to bake biscuits. So, pick your favorite.

In a mixing bowl, combine the baking powder, nutmeg, baking soda, flour, and salt.

In a second bowl, combine the egg and milk.

Dump the wet mixture into the dried one. Mix well.

Add the cheese gradually while stirring.

Make sure the texture of the batter is as expected. If not, play with the quantity of milk or flour and make it right.

Dump a large tablespoon full of the mixture on the baking sheet and repeat until the batter is gone.

Make you space out the lumps of batter as they will expand when cooking.

Bake for 20-25 minutes or until the biscuits are golden and done.

Brush the melted butter on the hot biscuits. Let them cool them before serving.

14. Sautéed Teriyaki Tofu

I never thought I would fee tofu to my toddler, and you certainly don't have to. But if you choose to, you want to use this recipe! I had a friend over one day who's a vegetarian. Also, I made this dish for her, and my toddler could not get enough of it!

Serving Size: 4-6

Cooking Time: 30 minutes

Ingredients:

- 1/3 cup teriyaki sauce
- 1 tbsp. soya sauce
- 2 tbsp. honey or maple syrup
- 1 tbs. sesame seeds
- ½ tsp. garlic powder
- ½ block of firm tofu (about 6 ounces)
- Sesame oil

Instructions:

Combine the sauces, spices, and honey or maple syrup in a medium plastic container.

Cut the firm tofu into cubes, triangles, or strips.

Place in the marinade and let it sit for about 15 minutes in the fridge.

Heat the sesame oil in a large pan and sauté the sesame seeds for a few minutes. Set them aside.

In the remaining oil, sauté the tofu pieces for 15 minutes total. Make sure you flip them and stir them, so they do not burn.

Serve warm to your toddlers. I usually serve white rice on the side with the tofu.

15. Ham, Pasta, Peas, and Ranch Sauce

Let's make this dish fun for both you and your toddler! I often make this basic pasta salad for the kids, but I leave the ranch sauce out for my portion, add a balsamic vinaigrette on mine, diced tomatoes, and Feta cheese. For the toddlers, stick to the original recipe but have them try yours. You never know!

Serving Size: 4-6

Cooking Time: 45 Minutes

Ingredients:

- ½ box of your chosen uncooked pasta (8 ounces)
- 1 cup sweet peas
- 2 Tbsp. Diced finely sweet onion
- ½ cup cubed smoked ham
- 1/3 cup ranch sauce, your favorite brand
- Pinch salt

Instructions:

Bring water to a boil in a medium pot.

Add the pasta and cook for 12 minutes or until done.

Drain the pasta.

Place in a large mixing bowl.

Gather all other ingredients and when the pasta has cooled down, add the ranch sauce and pinch of salt.

Combine well, and then add the onion, peas, and ham.

Stir again and taste before serving to your little one.

You could also add cubed Swiss cheese to this recipe.

16. French Toasts Topped with Strawberries

Toddlers like pancakes and French toasts. My toddler loves strawberries. Find your toddler's favorite fruit. It could be bananas, blueberries, or other top French toasts you just made with fresh fruits. Also, sprinkle some powdered sugar all over!

Serving Size: 2-3

Cooking Time: 20 Minutes

Ingredients:

- 3 slices of thick bread, your favorite o I should say your toddler's favorite
- 1 cup fresh sliced strawberries, or other favorite fruits
- 1 large egg
- ¾ cup almond milk
- ½ tbsp. almond extract
- Pinch ground cinnamon
- 1 tbsp. powdered sugar
- Unsalted butter

Instructions:

In a medium bowl, whisk the egg and add the milk, almond extract, and cinnamon. Combine well.

Heat the butter in a large pan, where all 3 slices of bread can fit.

Dip one slice at a time in the egg's mixture and lay in the hot buttery pan.

Cook for about 5 minutes on each side.

When nice and golden, serve fresh strawberries on tops and powdered sugar.

You can always add maple syrup or whipped cream also.

Don't forget to cut the French toast also in smaller bites, always easier for the toddlers to enjoy!

Serve with a glass of milk.

17. Banana and Chocolate Milkshake

Oh, if you want to create an impression on your toddler or anyone as a matter of fact, make a milkshake! Sure, you can make one using only chocolate and vanilla, but adding a banana will make it much more nutritious!

Serving Size: 1

Cooking Time: 10 Minutes

Ingredients:

- ½ tbsp. chocolate proteins powder
- 1 cup milk (it can be whole milk, almond milk, or even soy milk)
- ½ ripe banana
- A handful of chocolate chips

Instructions:

Combine the milk, protein powder, and banana in a high-speed blender.

Blend until you get a smooth texture.

If you find the mixture too thick, add a little milk and blend again.

Serve with a large colorful straw and sprinkle some chocolate chips on top.

18. Fun Beef Tacos in a Cup

Their little hands would like to hold these adorable cups and pick at what's inside. So, choose carefully what you put inside. You could use chicken or turkey ground meat, but generally, beef is a favorite.

Serving Size: 12

Cooking Time: 45 Minutes

Ingredients:

- ½ pound lean ground beef
- 1 tbsp. water
- ½ cup black beans, warmed
- ½ cup fresh shredded Iceberg lettuce
- 1 diced fresh tomato
- 2-3 tablespoons of sour cream
- ½ cup cheddar cheese
- 1 diced avocado
- ½ tbsp. minced garlic
- ½ tbsp. chili powder
- ½ tsp. onion powder
- 6 large tortilla breads
- A little olive oil

Instructions:

Preheat the oven to 350°F.

Grease a 12 holes muffin pan and set it aside.

In a large pan, heat some oil and cook the garlic for a few minutes.

Add the meat with water and all spices. Mix well and cook for about 15 minutes or until done.

Make sure you stir almost constantly, so the meat stays crumbly.

When done, drain all excess fat very well and set it aside.

Cut all tortilla breads in half.

Use each half to create a cup by folding it just so and fitting it in each muffin pan hole.

Add a generous tablespoon of meat and then sprinkle a teaspoon of cheese.

Place in the oven for 10-12 minutes or nil the cheese has melted nicely.

Remove from the oven and decorate with the toppings we listed (tomatoes, sour cream, diced avocado, lettuce, and warm beans).

Of course, leave out any that your toddler won't enjoy, or better yet, let them decide which one they want!

19. Beans Quesadillas with a Side of Sweet Peas

I think using beans to prepare your toddler's meal is a great idea. Beans contain proteins and iron, so super nutrition. Also, toddlers often don't mind their textures, and if they do, you can mash them and blend them with cheese.

Serving Size:2

Cooking Time: 20 Minutes

Ingredients:

- 1 large tortilla bread
- ¼ cup black beans or red kidney beans, depending on which one your family prefers
- 2/3 cup shredded Mozzarella cheese
- Frozen pea, as needed
- Little unsalted butter for cooking

Instructions:

Lay your tortilla bread down.

Spread generous portions of beans and cover with cheese.

Fold the tortilla bread in half.

Melt some butter in a large pan and lay the tortilla bread carefully.

Cook for about 7-8 minutes on this first side. Press a few times with a spatula.

Flip over, make sure the filling does not spill.

Press the other side also into the pan and cook another 5 minutes.

Remove from the heat and cut into triangles.

Warm some frozen peas or canned peas and serve on the side to add a nice green touch.

20. A Little Hardboiled Egg, A Little Guacamole, and a Little Cracker

What's next? Individual iconic ingredients to make a beautiful, yummy plate. Your toddler will be amused and impressed by these wonderful colors. Think about the white and yellow feature by a hardboiled egg cut in half. Add some guacamole, and you have quite a plate to feature.

Serving Size:2

Cooking Time: 15 minutes

Ingredients:

- 1 hardboiled egg
- 8 crackers of your choice
- ½ avocado, pitted
- Few drops of lemon juice
- Pinch salt

Instructions:

Make sure you save 1 hardboiled egg next time you prepare some for this easy meal.

You can make 2 for the toddlers with just 1 egg.

In a small bowl, mash the ½ fresh avocado and add a little salt and lemon juice.

Cut the hardboiled in half and then again in slices.

Get two plates out.

Display the sliced egg and then 4 crackers on each plate.

Spread a generous layer of guacamole on each cracker.

If you don't have 2 toddlers to serve, sit down and enjoy this snack lunch with your child.

21. Banana Splits Made Out of Granola and Fruits

Forget the high sugared chocolate and ice cream banana splits. Use some fresh fruits instead and some granola. Slice the bananas open and add these healthy ingredients, maybe a little cream or even homemade whipped cream.

Serving Size: 4

Cooking Time: 10 Minutes

Ingredients:

- 2 bananas medium ripped
- Few drops lemon juice
- ¼ cup granola mix
- 1 cup fresh berries of your choice (blueberries and raspberries look very pretty)
- Whipped cream

Instructions:

Peel the bananas and cut them lengthwise first.

Then each half needs to be cut again in half, wide-wise.

Brush a little lemon juice on the bananas, and this is to avoid them turning black because of oxidation.

Place 2 halves in a bowl and garnish with granola and fruits.

Add some whipped cream on top.

If you are serving this one for dessert, alright, you can serve with vanillas ice cream, no problem!

22. Is It an Owl or Is It a Bagel?

Even when it's not breakfast time, you can always create a breakfast dish for your hungry toddler. Use a bagel, a toast, or an English muffin and make it really fun. Use your imagination. Think of the bagel as a canvas and decorate it as a cute owl.

Serving Size: 1

Cooking Time: 10 Minutes

Ingredients:

- 1/2 plain bagel
- 2 slices of banana
- 1/2 tbsp. peanut butter or almond butter
- 1 sliced strawberry
- 1 green grape cut in half
- 4 blueberries

Instructions:

Place the half bagel in the toaster.

I listed plain bagel, but if your child likes cinnamon and raisins bagel, which is also a good option.

Once the bagel comes out of the toaster, spread with the creamy butter you picked.

Then it's decorating time! Ask your toddler to help.

But overall, it should go as follows: bananas will be the outside of the eyes, and then add the green grapes on top. Use 4 blueberries to make the mouth and then strawberries as the wings.

It does not matter too much what it looks like as long as you're having fun with your little one and that they are interested in eating this healthy breakfast or snack.

23. Thick and Yummy Veggies Soup

A vegetable soup needs to be thicker than usual for the toddlers to love it. Also, it can't be too spicy, as you know. Finally, make sure evidently, it's not too hot. If your soup checks all these boxes, you are in good shape!

Serving Size:4

Cooking Time: 50-60- Minutes

Ingredients:

- 1 large peeled and sliced carrot
- 1 large peeled and sliced white potatoes
- 1 can (8 ounces) of tomato soup
- 3 cups vegetables or chicken broth
- ½ cup kernel corn
- 1 tsp. Italian seasonings
- ¼ tsp. onion powder
- ¼ tsp. salt
- ¼ tsp. garlic powder
- ¼ cup sour cream
- Fresh parsley for garnishing

Instructions:

In a medium pot, boil water and salt.

Add the potato and carrot and cook for 10 minutes.

Drain and set aside.

In a high-speed blender, add potato, carrot, and the rest of the ingredients (except for the parsley), but only half of the sour cream.

Blend a few times until the texture is smooth, but you can still see some chunks in it.

Decorate with fresh parsley if you have some sour cream.

Help your toddlers eat their soup as needed.

24. Corn Muffins Filled with Hot Dog

I don't know if my toddler or myself gets more excited about this recipe! Of course, corn dogs are known and perfect for the fair, but you don't need to make them at home since they are deep-fried. Instead, follow this recipe!

Serving Size: 6-8

Cooking Time: 50-60 Minutes

Ingredients:

- 2 ½ cups cornmeal
- ½ tsp. baking powder
- ½ cup kernel corn
- 1 egg
- 3 hot dog sausages, I buy only 100% beef
- ½ cup whole milk
- ½ tsp. baking soda
- ¼ tsp. salt

Instructions:

Preheat your oven (350°F).

Grease a 12 cups muffin pan. Set aside.

Combine the baking soda, cornmeal, salt, and baking powder in a mixing bowl.

In a second bowl, combine the egg, milk, and corn.

Add the wet mixture into the dry one and combine well.

Cut the hot dogs into 4 pieces to make 12 total.

Fill half of each muffin hole with the mixture.

Add a piece of sausage and finish off with more batter.

Bake in the oven for 40 minutes.

Remove from the oven and let them sit and cool down.

Most toddlers will devour with some ketchup on the side to dip them in.

25. Chocolate Pudding and A Side of Berries

Toddlers are allowed to have desserts! I am suggested, however, to use a minimum of sugars within the recipe. Why not follow a Keto diet pudding recipe. Use avocado for texture, for example. Just try it!

Serving Size: 6-8

Cooking Time: 40-45 Minutes

Ingredients:

- 1 large avocado
- 1 tbsp. cocoa powder
- 2 ½ cups whole milk
- Pinch ground cinnamon
- Whipped cream when serving

Instructions:

Get your hand mixer out.

In a large bowl, mash the avocado. Add the milk and the cacao and use the hand mixer to get it to a very smooth texture.

Add the cinnamon and mix all over again.

Divide the mixture into ramequins and cover them.

Place in the refrigerator at least a few hours before serving.

Enjoy with whipped cream on top!

Conclusion

We know how important it is to feed your family healthy foods, especially your toddlers. We are glad you allowed us to help you on your journey.

Here are a few last valuable tips for the great parents you already are:

- Freeze leftovers in small portions, so it's ready for your toddler's meal.
- Make a list of meal options for your toddler, as you would for the family, so you won't revert to frozen pizzas at the last minute when you are tired.
- Invest in fun plastic colorful plates and silverware for your little one. Placemats also are very entertaining and help toddlers stay at the table or in their highchairs.
- Concerning behaviors will happen regarding your toddler's eating habits. They will love some food one day and want nothing to do with it the next. Don't worry too much, and it's a normal cycle. Keep introducing the food.
- Toddler's appetites often depend on their growth spurts. Also, of course, the activities they performed during the day. Again, don't worry too much if your kid is too tired from his playdate to eat properly a night here and there.
- If your toddler refuses to eat certain foods, again, don't force them. Just give them several healthy options (maybe offer broccoli vs. cauliflower or carrots vs. celery), keep showing them options. Your child is allowed to have likes and dislikes. Stay calm and be patient. Start by serving small portions to your child, and then add on.
- It's a good idea to let your toddler help with the food preparation. They can do a lot more than we sometimes give them credit for. Help with washing fruits and veggies. Stirring mixtures or even sprinkle toppings on salads.

- Don't forget to monitor how your child's eating habits are at daycare. Ask the teachers and request a copy of the menu as needed.

Enjoy your toddler, enjoy preparing his meals and enjoy watching him grow into a healthy child a little more every day.

Epilogues

There are days I feel like quitting, but then I remember readers like you, and my heart swells with pride at the love you show me by buying each and every book I put out there.

I am delighted, to say the least, to know that people like you take their time to download, read and cook with my books!

Thank you so much for accepting me and all that I have shared with the world.

While I am basking in the euphoria of your love and commitment to my books, I would beseech you to kindly drop your reviews and feedback. I would love to read from you!

Head to Amazon.com to drop your reviews!!!

Thank you

Charlotte Long

About the Author

For the past 10 years, Charlotte has been collating and exploring different dishes from different cultures of the world. Birthed and raised in Ohio, Charlotte grew up to know that cooking is a magical activity that requires a certain degree of commitment and love to be carried out.

She learnt this from her grandmother who was one of the best local chefs in Ohio then. Charlotte's grandmother would always create and invent new recipes and also refurbish old ones. The result of it is her passion for cooking cum a large book of special recipes that Charlotte inherited.

Using her grandmother's recipe book as her foundational training guide, Charlotte wore her grandmother's chef shoes to become one of the best chefs in Ohio and its environment.

Charlotte has written different recipe books, and she is currently touring the Caribbean and looking for new recipes to unravel.

Made in the USA
Monee, IL
11 June 2023

35614378R00037